WE DRIVE
Dumper Trucks

Ruby Tuesday Books

Alix Wood

Published in 2025 by Ruby Tuesday Books Ltd.

Copyright © 2025 Ruby Tuesday Books Ltd.

All rights reserved. No part of this publication may be reproduced in whole or in part, stored in any retrieval system, or transmitted in any form or by any means, electronic, mechanical, photocopying, recording, or otherwise, without written permission from the publisher.

Editors: Ruth Owen & Mark J. Sachner
Design & Production: Alix Wood

Photo credits:
Alamy: 14B (Stephen Barnes/Transport), 16 (Ashley Cooper pics), 20 (Deborah Howe); iStockPhoto: 3 (Miguel Perfectti), 8B (LordHenriVoton), 9 (Apriori1), 10T (Phynart Studio); Shutterstock: Cover (Mr. Tempter), 1 (igormakarov/Manop Boonpeng), 4 (Rob Wilson), 5 (MuchMania/WinWin artlab), 6 (aappp), 7T (Carolyn Franks), 7B (Olexa Misyachny), 8T (General Photographer), 10B (Tatiana Stulbo/Elena Istomina), 11 (Dmitry Kalinovsky), 12 (Deek), 13T (Darius Sul), 13B, 14T (Nerthuz), 15T (yanchi1984), 15B (Nerthuz), 17T (Alex Sobal), 17B (Tanes Ngamsom), 18 (M. Khebra), 19 (Miguel Perfectti), 21 (Maksim Safaniuk), 22T (Marius Dobilas), 22C (Another77), 22B (Rob Wilson), 23T (RobSt), 23C (RobSt), 23B (Vadim Ratnikov).

British Library Cataloguing in Publication Data (CIP) is available for this title.

ISBN 978-1-78856-587-5

Printed in Poland by L&C Printing Group

www.rubytuesdaybooks.com

Contents

Moving Mountains 4

Glossary 22

Index 24

Moving Mountains

Many vehicles work at a **building site**.

Dumper trucks are big, powerful vehicles that can carry away unwanted soil.

Dumper trucks also collect building materials, such as rock and sand, from **quarries**.

Then they deliver the materials to building sites.

BUILDING SITE →

Dumper trucks carry their load in a large container known as a **bed**.

Dumper trucks need big wheels and tyres to help carry their heavy loads.

Some dumper trucks have extra wheels.

Extra wheels

The driver can drop down the extra wheels when the bed has a heavy load.

Wheels up

Wheels down

Dumper truck drivers usually start work early.

First, they check that the truck is safe to drive.

Then they check where they need to go.

This driver's first job is to deliver some sand.

She drives to the sand quarry to collect it.

At the quarry, an excavator driver is waiting.

Excavator

The dumper truck driver reverses up to the excavator.

An excavator driver beeps their horn when the dumper truck is in the right spot.

Then the excavator starts to load the truck with sand.

The driver takes the load to where it is needed.

They park, and then press a button in the cab.

A ram lifts the back of the truck up into the air.

The sand starts to pour from the **tailgate**.

Some dumper trucks tip forwards instead of backwards.

Ram

Other trucks tip sideways.

Ram

Some dumper trucks are **articulated.**

The cab and the bed are joined by a hinge.

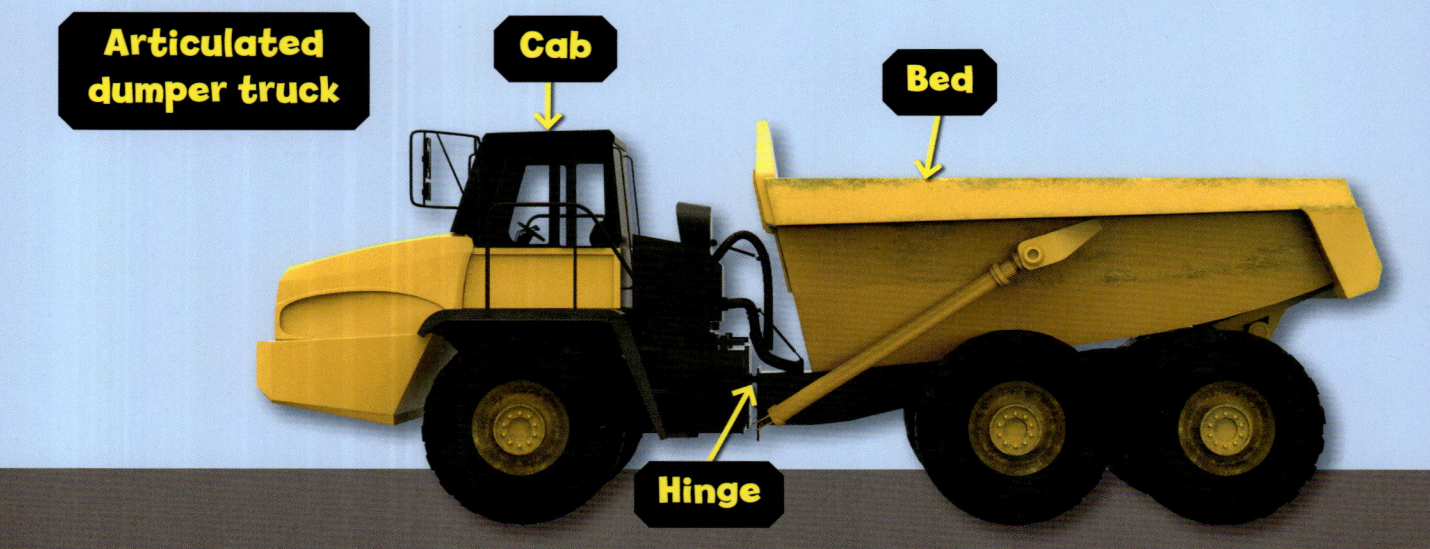

The hinge allows them to turn in small spaces.

On muddy or wet sites, drivers use dumper trucks with tracks.

The tracks help spread the weight so the truck doesn't sink into the ground.

Cab

Bed

Tracks

To move very large loads, drivers use a giant dumper truck.

These trucks are too big and heavy to drive on the road.

Giant dumper trucks have to be carried to a site by a big, powerful truck.

This is the largest dumper truck in the world.

The bed can carry the weight of three houses!

It has two engines.

Each wheel is taller than two people.

Giant dumper trucks are so tall the driver climbs a ladder up to the cab!

Giant dumper trucks are used in quarries.

They can carry huge loads of rock.

A giant excavator loads the rock.

Drivers use their mirrors and a camera to help them see as they reverse.

Drivers sometimes have to tip their load over the edge of a steep drop.

Mirrors

The camera is under here on the tailgate.

Steep drop

Skilful dumper truck drivers can even make their own roads!

They slowly pour out gravel as they drive backwards.

The wheels push the gravel into the ground.

When all the loads are delivered, a dumper truck driver's busy day is over.

Tomorrow they need to be back delivering loads again!

Glossary

articulated
Having a hinge or joint that allows a vehicle to turn easily.

bed
The part of a dumper truck that carries rock, sand or other materials.

Bed

building site
A piece of land where building work is taking place.

quarry
A large hole in the ground from which rock or other materials are dug.

ram
A tube with a strong rod inside that can push the bed upwards to dump a heavy load.

tailgate
A hinged panel or door on the back of a vehicle that can be opened to load or unload objects or materials.

Index

A
articulated dumper trucks 14

B
beds 6–7, 14–15, 17
building sites 4–5

E
excavators 4–5, 10–11, 18

G
giant dumper trucks 16–17, 18

Q
quarries 5, 9, 10, 18

R
rams 12–13

T
tailgates 12, 19
tipping (a load) 12–13, 19
tracks 15

W
wheels 6–7, 17, 20